Deaf and Hearing Impaired Pupils in Mainstream Schools

Linda Watson, Susan Gregory and Stephen Powers

D0165092

David Fulton Publishers
London

David Fulton Publishers Ltd
Ormond House, 26–27 Boswell Street, London WC1N 3JD

First published in Great Britain by David Fulton Publishers 1999

British Library Cataloguing in Publication Data
A catalogue record for this book is available from the British Library.

ISBN 1-85346-588-7

Typeset by Textype Typesetters, Cambridge
Printed in Great Britain by The Cromwell Press Ltd, Trowbridge, Wilts.

Contents

Contributors

Susan Gregory is Reader in Deaf Education, School of Education, University of Birmingham with responsibility for training Teachers of the Deaf. Her research interests include the development of deaf children and sign bilingual approaches to education.

Stephen Powers is Lecturer in Education, School of Education, University of Birmingham, with a primary responsibility for training Teachers of the Deaf. His research interests are educational attainments and inclusion.

Linda Watson is Lecturer in Education at the University of Birmingham, with responsibility for training Teachers of the Deaf. Her research interests include the oral/aural approach to the education of deaf children.

Acknowledgements

The authors would like to thank Sue Archbold for her assistance in compiling the case studies for the pupils with cochlear implants and Janet Little for her secretarial support.

Foreword

Each publication in this series of books is concerned with approaches to intervention with children with specific needs in mainstream schools. In this preface we provide a backdrop of general issues concerning special needs in mainstream schools. The government's recent Action Programme, published after considering responses to the Special Educational Needs (SEN) Green Paper, will lead to changes in practice in the future. Following consultation, there will be a revised and simplified Code of Practice in place by the school year 2000/2001. It is intended that this will make life easier.

The SEN Code of Practice (DfE 1994a), following the 1993 Education Act, provides practical guidance to LEAs and school governing bodies on their responsibilities towards pupils with SEN. Schools and LEAs were required to regard its recommendations from September 1994. The Department for Education also issued Circular 6/94 (DfE 1994b) which provided suggestions as to how schools should manage their special needs provision alongside that made by other local schools. These documents embody the twin strategies of individual pupil support and whole-school development. The Green Paper *Excellence for All* also seeks to promote the development of more sophisticated and comprehensive forms of regional and local planning (DfEE 1997).

The Code of Practice, with its staged approach to assessment supervised within each mainstream school by a teacher designated as Special Educational Needs Coordinator (SENCO), was widely welcomed.

For example, Walters (1994) argued that 'this Code of Practice builds on good practice developed over the ten years and heralds a "new deal" for children with special needs in the schools of England and Wales'. But he also reflected worries that, in the light of other developments, the process might provide an added incentive for schools to dump their 'problem children into the lap of the LEA' rather than devising strategies to improve behaviour in the school environment. Such children, he feared, were in danger of being increasingly marginalised.

Impact on teachers

While receiving a mainly positive welcome for its intentions, the Code of Practice (DfE 1994a) also raised some concerns about its impact on teachers who became responsible for its implementation. On the positive side the Code would raise the profile of special needs and establish a continuum of provision in mainstream schools. There was a clear specification of different types of special educational need and the Code's emphasis was on meeting them through individual programmes developed in cooperation with parents.

However, there were possible problems in meeting the challenge of establishing effective and time-efficient procedures for assessment and monitoring. Further challenges were to be found in making best use of resources and overcoming barriers to liaison with parents.

Anxieties about the Code

Following the introduction of the Code these anxieties were confirmed by a number of research studies of teachers' perceptions of the impact of the Code. The picture which emerged from these studies showed appreciation of the potential benefits of implementing the Code but widespread anxiety, based on early experience, about the practicalities of making it work.

Loxley and Bines (1995) interviewed head teachers and SENCOs about their views on emergent issues related to the complexities of introducing Individual Education Plans (IEPs), particularly in secondary schools.

Teachers feared that 'excessive proceduralism' could lead to the distribution of resources being skewed towards meeting the needs of children whose parents are best able to understand and exercise their rights, at the expense of provision for children whose parents are less assertive and confident. Teachers were most concerned about the allocation of scarce resources and the increased responsibilities of SENCOs for managing a system likely to reduce time for direct teaching of children.

School perspectives

Most schools were optimistic about their ability to implement the Code and positive about LEA guidelines and training, but there was less certainty that the Code would improve the education of pupils with SEN.

Asked to give their opinion on advantages and disadvantages of the Code, teachers cited as positive effects:

- a more structured framework,
- growing awareness of accountability,
- a higher profile for SEN issues,
- earlier identification,
- greater uniformity in practice, and
- increased parental involvement.

The disadvantages cited were:

- lack of resources and time,
- substantially increased workloads for all teachers as well as SENCOs,
- more time used for liaison and less for teaching.

(Rhodes 1996)

Four themes

A national survey commissioned by the National Union of Teachers (NUT) identified four themes:

1. broad support for the principles and establishment of the Code of Practice;
2. concern about the feasibility of its implementation, given a lack of time and resources;
3. problems in some areas related to perceived inadequacy of LEA support;
4. inadequate status and lack of recognition for the SENCO role.

(Lewis *et al.* 1996)

Another study found patchy support for SENCOs. There were wide variations in the amount of time dedicated to the role, the amount of support from head teachers and governors, involvement in decision-making, the extent of training and the degree of bureaucracy within LEAs.

SEN Register and Staged Assessment Procedures

Although its widespread adoption makes it appear to have been a national prescription, the five-stage model suggested in the Code is not a legal requirement. The Code actually states that: 'to give specific help to children who have special educational needs, schools should adopt a staged response'. (DfE 1994a, 2.20)

It goes on to indicate that some schools and LEAs may adopt different models but that, while it was not essential that there should be five stages, it was essential that there should be differentiation between the stages, aimed at matching action taken to the pupil's needs at each stage.

Five Key Stages

Nonetheless, the normal expectation is that assessment and intervention will be organised and recorded in an SEN Register for which the SENCO is responsible. The following description briefly summarises usual practice, with Stages 1-3 school-based and Stages 4 and 5 the responsibility of the LEA.

Stage 1
Class teacher identifies pupils with learning difficulty and, with support from the SENCO, attempts to meet the pupil's SEN.

Stage 2
Class teacher reports continued concern and SENCO takes responsibility for the special response to meet the pupil's SEN.

Stage 3
SENCO organises support from external agencies to help in meeting the pupil's SEN.

Stage 4
The LEA is approached by the school with a request for statutory assessment.

Stage 5
The LEA considers the need for a Statement of SEN and completes the assessment procedure; monitoring and review of the statement is organised by the LEA.

Each book in this series, explains how this process works in relation to different disabilities and difficulties as they were described in the 1981 Act and shows how individual needs can be identified and met through IEPs. While forthcoming revision of the Code may alter the details of the stages, the principles of the practices through which needs are specified will remain the same.

Information for colleagues, governors and parents

Ensuring that the school provides all necessary information for staff, governors and parents is another major element of the SENCO role. *The Organisation of Special Educational Provision* (Circular 6/94) (DfE 1994b) sets out the issues which the school should address about its SEN provision, policies and partnerships with bodies beyond the school.

This is information that must be made available and may be found in school brochures or prospectuses, in annual reports to parents and in policy documents. The ultimate responsibility for following the guidance in the Circular rests with the head teacher and governing body but the SENCO will be engaged with all these issues and the Circular forms in effect a useful checklist for monitoring the development and implementation of the SEN policy.

You may find it useful to consider the following points as a way of familiarising yourself with provision in your school.

Basic information about the school's special educational provision

- Who is responsible for co-ordinating the day-to-day provision of education for pupils with SEN at your school (whether or not the person is known as the SEN Co-ordinator)?
- Arrangements need to be made for coordinating the provision of education for pupils with SEN. Does your school's SENCO work alone or is there a coordinating or support team?
- What are the admission arrangements for pupils with SEN who do not have a statement and is there any priority for SEN admissions?
- What kind of provision does your school have for the special educational needs in which it specialises?
- What are your school's access arrangements for pupils with physical and sensory disabilities?

Information about the school's policies for the identification, assessment and provision for all pupils with SEN

- What is your school policy on allocation of money for SEN resources?
- How are pupils with SEN identified and their needs determined and reviewed? How are parents told about this?
- What does your school policy say about arrangements for providing access for pupils with SEN to a balanced and broadly-based curriculum (including the National Curriculum)?
- What does your school policy say about 'integration arrangements'? How do pupils with SEN engage in the activities of the school together with pupils who do not have special educational needs.
- How does your school demonstrate the effective implementation of its SEN policy? How does the governing body evaluate the success of the education which is provided at the school for pupils with SEN?
- What are the arrangements made by the governing body relating to the treatment of complaints from parents of pupils with SEN concerning the provision made at the school?
- What are your school's 'time targets' for response to complaints?

Information about the school's staffing policies and partnership with bodies beyond the school

- What is your school's policy on continuing in-service professional training for staff in relation to special educational needs?
- What are your school's arrangements regarding the use of teachers and facilities from outside the school, including links with support services for special educational needs?

- What is the role played by the parents of pupils with SEN? Is there a 'close working relationship'?
- Do you have any links with other schools, including special schools, and is there provision made for the transition of pupils with SEN between schools or between the school and the next stage of life or education?
- How well does 'liaison and information exchange' work in your school, e.g. links with health services, social services and educational welfare services and any voluntary organisations which work on behalf of children with SEN?

In any school those arrangements which are generally available to meet children's learning needs will have an impact on those services which are required to meet specific needs. It is therefore very important that a reader of any one of this series of specialist books makes reference to the general situation in their school when thinking about ways of improving the learning situation for pupils.

Harry Daniels and Colin Smith
The University of Birmingham
February 1999

References

Crowther, D., Dyson, A. *et al.* (1997) *Implementation of the Code of Practice: The Role of the Special Educational Needs Co-ordinator.* Special Needs Research Centre, Department of Education, University of Newcastle upon Tyne.

Department for Education (DfE) (1994a) *Code of Practice on the Identification and Assessment of Special Educational Needs.* London: HMSO.

Department for Education (DfE) (1994b) *The Organisation of Special Educational Provision.* Circular 6/94. London: HMSO.

Department for Education and Employment (DfEE) (1997) *Excellence for All: Meeting Special Educational Needs.* London: HMSO.

Hornby, G. (1995) 'The Code of Practice: boon or burden', *British Journal of Special Education* 22(3) 116–119.

Lewis, A., Neill, S. R. St J., Campbell, R. J. (1996) *The Implementation of the Code of Practice in Primary and Secondary Schools: A National Survey of the Perceptions of Special Educational Needs Co-ordinators.* The University of Warwick.

Loxley, A. and Bines, H. (1995) 'Implementing the Code of Practice: professional responses', *Support for Learning* 10(4) 185-189.

Rhodes, L. W. (1996) 'Code of Practice: first impressions', *Special!* Spring, 1996.

Walters, B. (1994) *Management of Special Needs.* London: Cassell.

CHAPTER 1

Introduction: the range of deaf and hearing impaired pupils

Linda Watson

The majority of pupils who are deaf or hearing impaired are educated in mainstream classes. This means that mainstream teachers will not only come into contact with these pupils, but will have the responsibility for teaching them. Given the many demands made on mainstream teachers in terms of delivering the National Curriculum, coping with the implementation of innovative policies such as the National Literacy Strategy and ensuring that their school's SATs results are improving, not to mention surviving the rigours of OFSTED inspections, to expect them also to cater appropriately for pupils with special educational needs could be seen as asking too much. Yet many mainstream teachers are enthusiastic about the policy of including all pupils in mainstream schools and see the benefits of such placements. A positive attitude, while it is a good starting point, however, is not sufficient of itself to ensure that the special educational needs of specific groups of pupils are met and this book aims to give some guidance in meeting the needs of deaf and hearing impaired pupils.

There is a wide range of pupils covered by the title of the book, as will become apparent from the following chapters. Some deaf pupils will wear hearing aids, some will have a fluctuating hearing loss, and others will prefer to communicate using sign language. If this book succeeds in giving mainstream teachers, learning support assistants and others who may meet deaf and hearing impaired pupils in school a greater understanding not only of the difficulties which these pupils may face but also of the contribution which they can make to the school then it will have fulfilled its aim.

It is not a book on anatomy and physiology. The workings of the ear will not be discussed in detail, although some reference will be made where this is relevant to the way in which sound passes through the ear and is perceived by the brain. Readers who wish to make a more detailed study of this area should consult a basic text on the subject, suggestions for which are listed at the end of the book. Neither is the book intended as an introduction to hearing aids, radio hearing aids, classroom FM systems, cochlear implants or other forms of amplification equipment which may be found in mainstream schools and used by deaf and hearing impaired pupils. Rather it is a book about how to ensure both that the needs of these pupils are met and that they are encouraged to contribute fully to the life of the school. Much is currently being said about including all pupils in mainstream schools, but if it is to be true inclusion then all pupils, including those pupils with special educational needs, must be seen as valued and contributing members of the school. It is hoped that, through explanation, examples and case studies, misconceptions and assumptions can be challenged and deaf and hearing impaired pupils empowered to fulfil their potential and participate fully in the life of the school.

Terminology

The terminology used in discussing deaf and hearing impaired pupils is complicated and merits some explanation. The title of this book may sound as if it refers to two distinct groups, but in actual fact the position is more complicated even than the title might suggest. Using the title 'deaf and hearing impaired' is intended to include all pupils with hearing loss. Some pupils will prefer to be referred to as 'deaf', while others will choose the term 'hearing impaired'. Those who choose to use the term 'deaf' may not have a more significant hearing loss than others who choose the term 'hearing impaired'. Some deaf people describe themselves as a minority group with their own language (British Sign Language (BSL)) and their own culture. For these people their deafness is seen in a positive light and they frequently choose to describe themselves as Deaf, with the capital D used to denote their identity as part of the Deaf community, i.e. those who share a common language and culture. This topic will be addressed in more detail in Chapter 4, which discusses those pupils for whom British Sign Language is their first language and others who find their identity with other deaf people who sign.

Other pupils may prefer the term 'hearing impaired'. When this term was introduced it was thought that it was a more positive term than 'deaf' as it emphasised the fact that the pupils had some hearing which could be useful to them. In the current climate, any term which includes the word 'impaired' or 'impairment' may be seen as negative, as is a term such as 'hearing loss' which stresses the element that is not present. This makes some deaf pupils reject these terms, preferring to assert that their deafness is a positive attribute. Other pupils, however, prefer the term 'hearing impaired' as they do not want to be classed as deaf. They find their friends and identity with hearing pupils and do not wish to be considered part of the Deaf community. Yet others may prefer the term 'deaf', feeling that it emphasises the degree of their hearing loss, but still reject any association with the Deaf community. This demonstrates how complicated the issue has become. Teachers of the Deaf have retained their name throughout and deal with pupils with the full range of hearing loss. The important point is that teachers should adopt the terminology which is preferred by pupils and parents and be aware that some pupils may react against certain words.

The term 'hard of hearing' is most commonly applied to adults who are losing their hearing in later life. However, it has recently been introduced in relation to children in some areas and may be seen as a useful term to describe children with mild hearing losses.

In this book the terms 'deaf' and 'hearing impaired' are sometimes used interchangeably, for instance in discussing pupils with conductive hearing loss. In other chapters, however, the term 'deaf' is used to refer to the whole range of hearing loss. This reflects common practice in the field of education of the deaf and also the personal preference of the authors.

Degree of hearing loss

Having discussed the terms by which individuals may prefer to describe themselves, there is other relevant terminology which it is useful to understand. Firstly, the degree of hearing loss. This is measured by comparison with 'normal' hearing and is expressed as mild, moderate, severe or profound. When hearing is tested using an audiometer, that is by presenting single sounds via headphones and noting the level at which the child can detect the sounds (the threshold), the results are plotted on a graph called an audiogram. The more severe the loss, the lower the graph will be plotted on the audiogram. Sometimes the result is quoted as an average, for example an average loss of 50 decibels (dB) would be classed as moderate whilst 80 dB would be termed severe. Other terms may also be used. For example, a hearing loss may be described as 'flat' if it affects low and high sounds equally, alternatively it may be described as a 'high frequency' loss if it affects mainly the higher sounds which are measured. These terms are significant in the effects that they are likely to have on the pupil's ability to discriminate speech. While a flat loss may appear more significant and produce a lower average, it is often possible to compensate more adequately for such a loss with a hearing aid by comparison with a high frequency loss which may not give such a low average but may have a very significant effect on the pupil's ability to hear speech. This is because the consonant sounds of speech are mainly high frequency and they carry most of the information, so a pupil with a high frequency hearing loss may miss many vital parts of words. This topic is covered again in relation to pupils with hearing aids in Chapter 3.

Type of hearing loss

Then there is the type of hearing loss, which is related to the cause. Many young children suffer from a type of hearing loss commonly known as 'glue ear'. This is a fluctuating condition, the effects of which can be so significant that the whole of Chapter 2 is devoted to it. Since this type of loss results from some interruption in the way that sound passes, or is conducted, through the outer or middle ear, caused by inflammation or fluid in the middle ear, it is known as a 'conductive' hearing loss. This is also the term used to describe the type of hearing loss resulting from a malformation of the ear (some children are born with the outer structure of the ear, which is commonly called the ear, but more precisely known as the pinna, either absent or only partly formed). A conductive loss may be amenable to surgery or may resolve itself, although this is not always the case.

The other type of hearing loss is called a 'sensori-neural' hearing loss. This is a permanent hearing loss, resulting from a problem in the inner ear, or cochlea, or in the nerve of hearing. Children may be born with a sensori-neural hearing loss. The cause may be a problem during pregnancy, for example if the mother has rubella (German measles) while she is pregnant; it may result from problems around the time of birth, for example babies born very prematurely or with very low birth weight may develop a hearing loss; but most commonly there is no obvious cause. In this case it is usually presumed that the cause of the hearing loss is genetic, in other words it was inherited from the parents. Both parents can be carriers of a recessive gene for deafness without being aware of it as they have normal hearing, it is only when they have a child who is deaf that they discover that they are carriers of the gene for deafness.

Some children develop a hearing loss after birth. The most common cause of this acquired deafness is meningitis, which can leave the child with a profound hearing loss. Another cause can be mumps, which usually only affects one ear. With the introduction of the measles, mumps and rubella (MMR) vaccination and the vaccination against one form of meningitis, the number of children with hearing loss resulting from these causes should decline.

Unilateral hearing loss

A hearing loss may be described as 'bilateral' or 'unilateral' (the term 'monaural' is sometimes used in place of unilateral). This refers to whether the loss affects both ears (bilateral) or only one ear (unilateral or monaural). The effects of a unilateral loss are not nearly as significant as those of a bilateral loss, in fact in some cases a unilateral loss is only detected as the result of a hearing test. Since this book does not have a chapter devoted to unilateral hearing loss, it seems appropriate to offer some advice at this point.

As already stated, some children do not seem to be very disadvantaged by a unilateral hearing loss. Whether they were born with it or acquired it, they seem to adapt to it. In good listening conditions they may seem to hear as well as other children, although careful observation may reveal that they are inclined to turn their head slightly so that their 'good' ear is turned towards the speaker. When conditions are not as favourable, however, they may experience difficulty. Some pupils with a unilateral loss who have not found it a problem previously may find that they are unable to follow a lesson or assessment presented via a tape recorder and they may need special arrangements such as the provision of a personal tape recorder or a live voice presentation of the material to be made for them at this stage. They may also need to check with a neighbour that they have got the correct page or for other precise information and such behaviour should not be discouraged as it is essential, even if checking serves mainly to increase their confidence.

We use the fact that we have two ears to aid us in detecting the source of a sound and in listening in noisy conditions. A sound which is directly in front of us or behind us will reach both ears simultaneously, whereas a sound to one side will reach the nearer ear fractionally before it reaches the ear farther away and will be slightly louder at the nearer ear. The brain is able to detect these very slight differences in timing and loudness and uses them to pinpoint the source of the sound. Where there is background noise present, the brain enables us to suppress the unwanted background noise being heard in one ear and to concentrate on the sound we want to hear. Again, the fact that we have two ears is important. Children with a unilateral hearing loss do not have this advantage of using the different information in each ear to assist them in detecting the source of sound or in listening in noisy conditions. For this reason, some thought needs to be given to their seating position in class. Older pupils should be able to assume this responsibility themselves, but younger pupils may need help. A position in which the good ear is towards the teacher is recommended. These pupils may also benefit from being able to look at the person, teacher or pupil, who is speaking in order to get additional information from their facial expression and lip patterns (speech reading). Bearing these facts in mind, the most advantageous position is usually towards the front of the class to one side with the good ear towards the class. This will allow the pupil to see the teacher and to turn and look at other pupils when they are speaking. A seating position directly in front of the teacher may not be as helpful, particularly if other pupils are going to contribute to the lesson as it will involve the pupil with a unilateral hearing loss in a great deal of turning to see other pupils.

A few pupils with unilateral hearing loss seem to be very disadvantaged by it. These may be pupils who have other difficulties, the effects of which are compounded by the presence of the unilateral loss. As we listen to speech we anticipate the words that might follow and this helps us. If we are unable to hear every word clearly we can still detect the message. This is because of our knowledge of the language. Pupils whose language development is delayed are likely to find more difficulty in hearing in adverse conditions since they will not have the same level of knowledge of the language to help them. For such pupils it is even more important that attention should be given to their seating position. It may also be necessary to employ some of the strategies mentioned elsewhere in the book in the chapters dealing with pupils with conductive hearing loss and those who are using hearing aids.

How to use this book

Each chapter of the book deals with a different group of pupils. While many readers will want to read the book in its entirety, others may prefer to identify the group into which the pupils with whom they are concerned fit and read that chapter first. Each chapter stands alone and the format of individual chapters varies.

Chapter 2 is concerned with the large group of pupils, particularly at Key Stage 1 (i.e. aged 5 to 7 years), who suffer from bouts of conductive hearing loss. It also includes children with mild hearing loss that is permanent in nature.

Chapter 3 discusses those pupils who use hearing aids and other forms of amplification but not any form of signing. The majority of deaf pupils who are integrated into mainstream schools fall into this category. This is the most detailed chapter and contains many points which apply to all deaf pupils regardless of their type or degree of deafness or whether they communicate purely orally or using some signs as well.

The contents of Chapter 4 cover those pupils who use sign language, either with or without the use of hearing aids. These pupils used to be educated almost exclusively in segregated schools or units, but are increasingly to be found in mainstream schools. The chapter also discusses deaf pupils who use both BSL and English in school. Their first, or preferred, language may be BSL or English.

Finally, Chapter 5 addresses the particular needs of deaf pupils who have been fitted with cochlear implants. This is a new form of hearing aid that is inserted surgically into the cochlea. The needs of this small but growing group of pupils merit their own chapter.

CHAPTER 2
Pupils with conductive hearing loss

Linda Watson

Michael

Michael is 7 and was born without a pinna on the right but with a normal ear on the left. On the right side of his face there were two flaps (or tags) of skin which were surgically removed within a few weeks of birth. His hearing was tested and found to be within normal limits on the left, with a moderate loss on the right. As he has normal hearing in one ear, it was decided not to attempt to open the canal on the right or to prescribe a hearing aid. His parents (and, as soon as he was able to understand, Michael himself) were advised that it was essential to conserve the hearing in his good ear, which meant that any infection should be treated immediately and he should be sure to wear ear protection if he engaged in any noisy sport, e.g. shooting or operated any noisy machines. At a recent appointment with the ENT consultant Michael was invited to consider whether he wanted to have a false pinna attached in place of the absent one for cosmetic purposes. He was able to meet some other children and adults who had been born with similar conditions, some of whom decided that they would like a prosthesis and others that they would prefer to simply wear their hair so that it covered the place where the pinna should have been. Michael decided that, for the time being at least, he would leave it.

In school Michael is able to take responsibility for ensuring that he sits with his good ear towards the teacher and in a position that enables him to see other pupils. In group work his group frequently chooses to work in a quiet area off the main classroom, which means that Michael can hear more easily. His teacher is aware of the situation and checks periodically that Michael is responding appropriately.

Annette

Annette is 5 and she was born with a pinna on each side but both ear canals were closed over. Her hearing was tested and she was found to have a moderate loss in both ears. Initially her parents were advised to make sure that they were close to her when talking to her; to speak clearly without shouting or over-emphasising and to keep background noise down. As the loss was only moderate and her parents were able to heed the advice, her language started to develop.

At one year it was decided that she would benefit from a hearing aid, particularly as she was starting to move around so it would be more difficult to talk to her from close range and she would need to hear other children clearly when she started to play with them. It was not possible to fit a postaural aid as there was no canal for the ear mould to fit into. She was fitted with a bone conduction hearing aid. The small vibrator fitted onto the mastoid behind one ear and was held in place by a headband to which it was attached and which also held the hearing aid. She tolerated the aid quite well, although it could be uncomfortable at times as it needed to be held very firmly against her mastoid bone in order for the sound to be transmitted. When she was eighteen months old, the ENT consultant suggested that he should open one ear canal surgically. This was successful and meant that she could now wear a postaural hearing aid as the mould would fit into her ear. However, the bone conduction aid was retained to wear if the ear got sore or became infected. Some months later the surgeon repeated the process on the other ear. This meant that Annette could now wear two postaural aids which enabled her to hear more clearly and to locate the source of sounds. If there was a problem with one ear she could still wear the aid in the other ear. The bone conduction aid had not been needed since the second operation but was retained for use should both ears become sore or infected at the same time.

When Annette started school her language development was on a par with the other children and her speech was totally intelligible. She needed some help initially with managing her hearing aids. The classroom assistant received instruction in checking the aids and replacing dud batteries. Her class teacher ensured that Annette was placed so that she could see and hear well. She received some extra one-to-one work to reinforce the phonic work and other early literacy skills and with this help was progressing at the same rate as the other pupils.

Conductive hearing loss is a term used to describe any hearing loss which results from an interference with the way in which sound travels through the outer or middle ear. In a healthy ear sound is collected by the outer ear, or pinna to give it its correct name, it then hits the eardrum sending it into vibration. These vibrations cause the three tiny bones in the middle ear, which is filled with air, to vibrate. The last of these three bones, commonly known as the stapes, or stirrup, is attached to the oval window which leads to the cochlea or inner ear. As the oval window is set into vibration it excites fluid in the inner ear which causes tiny hair cells to move, which in turn transmit nerve impulses along the auditory nerve to the brain where they are perceived as sound. This is a very simplified explanation of the working of the ear, for a more detailed description the reader is referred to one of the volumes listed at the end of the book.

There are several ways in which this passage of sound to the inner ear can be disturbed. The first is if there is no pinna. Some children are born without an external ear. In humans the pinna does not serve as important a function as in some other animals which are able to move their pinnas in order to locate the source of a sound. The absence of a pinna alone does not usually give rise to a very significant hearing loss, indeed the loss may be negligible. However, it is frequently accompanied by other abnormalities, for instance the ear canal, which leads to the eardrum, may be occluded (closed over); the middle ear cavity may be absent or the ossicles (the three tiny bones) may be absent or malformed. Even if all these symptoms occur together, however, the degree of hearing loss, while significant, is not usually as severe as a loss arising from a problem in the inner ear since it is the inner ear which serves the most important function in hearing.

If a child is born with a malformed or absent pinna, then the problem is immediately obvious. Checks are likely to be made on the child's hearing shortly after birth. A referral will be made to an ENT consultant and any necessary surgery, such as opening up the ear canal, will be decided upon and performed at an appropriate age. The parents will be aware that there may be some degree of hearing loss and offered advice on managing the environment and their interactions with the child to allow for this. If it becomes clear that the prescription of a hearing aid would be beneficial, then frequently it will be necessary to fit the child with either a bone conduction hearing aid or an in-the-ear aid. If there is no canal or no pinna, then it is not possible to fit a conventional hearing aid which has an ear mould which is custom-made to fit the child's ear canal and which sits on the pinna (a postaural or behind-the-ear aid). In this case the child may be fitted with a bone conduction hearing aid. This comprises a small vibrator which is held in place on the mastoid bone, behind the child's ear, by a headband, and a postaural hearing aid. If it is clear that this will be a long-term situation, then a small stud is surgically implanted behind the child's ear to which the aid is anchored to remove the necessity for a headband. A bone conduction aid may also be prescribed if a child's ears have a permanent discharge.

For a child who is born with an occluded ear canal, the surgeon may be able to open the canal surgically. The child may then be prescribed a hearing aid which fits into the canal. In addition to helping the child to hear, this also serves to keep the canal patent and is another way around the problem of a lack of pinna to hold a hearing aid.

Glue ear

By far the largest group of children affected by conductive hearing problems are those suffering from what is commonly known as 'glue ear'. There are actually various forms of otitis media with effusion (OME), to give the condition its correct name, with different causes. For the purposes of this chapter it is discussed as a single condition. The interested reader is referred to more detailed accounts elsewhere.

Lucy

Lucy is 5. When she started school her parents explained that she was prone to ear infections, having had four, all of which had followed from other infections, for example a severe cold. Her parents knew the symptoms and got an emergency appointment with their GP when they occurred. The GP prescribed antibiotics which reduced the inflammation. On the first occasion Lucy's eardrum had burst as a result of the acute infection, but this had healed. They were to keen to get the necessary treatment early enough to prevent a recurrence of this.

Following each ear infection Lucy's hearing had been adversely affected for four to six weeks. She was referred to the Child Hearing Clinic where the physician recommended that they keep a regular check on her hearing and that her parents should maintain a watchful eye on her health and hearing levels. They were given a leaflet offering advice on encouraging Lucy's language development, particularly on encouraging her to learn to listen again once her hearing returned to normal.

As a result Lucy's language development was above average for her age and her early literacy skills were developing. Her class teacher was on the alert for any warning signs that Lucy might be developing an ear infection and promised to inform her parents if she noticed any signs that Lucy might not be hearing well.

Many young children are prone to ear infections. Some children develop an ear infection after a cold or other infection, while in others the first symptom is the acute pain of an ear infection. In essence, the middle ear, which is usually filled with air, becomes filled with fluid which seeps into it from its mucous lining. This makes it harder for the eardrum to vibrate and also for the three bones in the middle ear to move, resulting in some degree of hearing loss. The whole area can become inflamed (acute otitis media) and require antibiotics, or the fluid may be present without any obvious medical symptoms.

In many children the condition rights itself in due course, although it may take several weeks, and the hearing returns to normal. In other children, however, the fluid does not drain away but rather becomes thicker and more viscous, hence the term 'glue ear' which accurately describes its consistency. This thick fluid is usually best removed by making a small surgical incision in the eardrum (a myringotomy) and draining the fluid out. A tiny washer (a grommet) may be inserted in the site of the myringotomy. This is in order to allow air to flow in and out of the middle ear, a function which is usually performed by the eustachian tube. In the case of glue ear the eustachian tube is blocked and so unable to allow the passage of air into the middle ear. The grommet is designed to work itself out after some weeks or months when hopefully the problem has resolved itself.

Some children suffer just one bout of glue ear and are very much helped by grommets. For other children, however, the problem continues, requiring more than one operation. There are differences of opinion among doctors and surgeons concerned with the treatment of children with glue ear. A standard treatment used to be to try decongestant medicine, but this had an adverse effect on some children and was not found to be efficacious in many cases. Some surgeons are reluctant to operate, preferring to wait for the child to outgrow the condition, while others are much more ready to perform repeated operations if necessary. Those surgeons who do not favour operating may suggest that children are prescribed hearing aids as a temporary measure.

Leaving aside the options on treatment, the implications for the teacher are both significant and difficult to comprehend. Firstly, it should be borne in mind that large numbers of young children may be affected. Estimates vary, but studies have found that at any one time nearly 20 per cent of children in the age range two to five years will be affected. This shows how common the condition is. Children who attend nurseries are more prone to ear infections and therefore to developing glue ear during the nursery years. It is more common during the winter months, although some children suffer all year round, possibly owing to allergies. There is evidence of a second peak in the numbers of children affected at around five years, which corresponds to the time when children start school and are possibly exposed to more infections.

Given the large number of children who suffer from OME to give it its medical term, it is important for teachers, particularly those involved with young children, to understand something about the condition. It has been found that the majority of children will suffer at least one bout of otitis media in their early years, but it is clear that not all children are adversely affected by it. The fact that some children do not seem to be noticeably affected either in educational terms or with respect to language development or behaviour has encouraged some ENT consultants in their belief that children should be allowed simply to outgrow the condition. It is true that it is mainly a disease of early childhood and most children will outgrow it by the end of Key Stage 1. However, for some children the effects are very significant. There may be several reasons for this, so each case should be considered individually.

Alex

Alex is 6 and has a history of upper respiratory tract infections and ear infections. His mother reports that he failed his health visitor hearing test at eight months, having already had one ear infection. Since then he has been under the care of an ENT consultant and attended the audiology clinic on a regular basis, where his hearing levels are monitored. After having a hearing loss for several months as a result of fluid which did not clear, he was put on the waiting list at two years six months for myringotomies to drain the fluid, the insertion of grommets to aerate his middle ears and removal of his adenoids since it was thought that these were contributing to the problem. He was called for the operation eleven months later, but unfortunately had an ear infection at the time so the operation had to be postponed. It was eventually carried out three months later. His family noticed an improvement in Alex's hearing and his speech began to improve. After only six weeks he had another ear infection and the grommet on one side was extruded. Two months later he had an infection in the other ear and his hearing returned to the level before the operation.

His parents took Alex to an allergy clinic where they were advised to give up smoking and not to allow Alex to swim in a swimming pool as the chlorine could set up an allergic reaction.

Eighteen months after the insertion of the first grommets the operation was repeated and tubes were inserted instead of grommets, in the hope that they would stay in for longer. By this time Alex was already in school where he was finding some difficulty in conforming to the expected patterns of behaviour, for example he wandered off during story time. He tended to use a very loud voice and his attention span was short. His speech was indistinct, his language development was delayed and he was slow to make a start at literacy.

The class teacher was concerned about Alex and his name was placed on the special needs register. Advice was sought from the school's Special Needs Coordinator (SENCO). Alex had previously been referred to the Speech and Language Therapist but had failed to keep appointments. The Speech and Language Therapist was invited to assess Alex in school, and found that his receptive and expressive language were both delayed by approximately two years and that his sound system was not yet fully developed. She agreed to monitor his progress.

As the school staff were very concerned the SENCO contacted the local Service for Hearing Impaired Children for advice. The visiting Teacher of the Deaf saw Alex in school. He explained that the Service does not see children with conductive hearing loss resulting from glue ear for regular support. However, he agreed to assess Alex and give advice. He observed Alex in the class and worked with him on a one-to-one basis. He found that, although Alex's hearing levels were now within normal limits he was not discriminating speech sounds clearly. This was more pronounced in the classroom. He recommended that Alex be given some activities which required accurate listening and that he be rewarded for accurate discrimination and given confidence that he could now hear. He suggested that as an interim measure the classroom assistant should share the story for story time with Alex individually prior to the session in the hope that he would find it easier to follow in class and therefore attend to the story which would give the desired improvement in his behaviour. He further recommended that Alex be given plenty of opportunity to develop his language skills in one-to-one and small group settings, in a relaxed atmosphere.

With regard to literacy it seemed that Alex needed help with the 'bottom up' skills. These would be helped by the listening activities as well as by direct work on reading-related activities. Alex was lacking in confidence in reading and possibly feeling a sense of failure. Reading stories which were very familiar so that he could anticipate the text with a high degree of accuracy and complete the whole book at one sitting should increase his confidence and sense of achievement.

It has been found that the effects of glue ear are likely to be more pervasive if there are already other adverse conditions. For example, children from less privileged backgrounds, whose language development is delayed by comparison with other children of the same age and who possibly do not experience sharing books and stories with an adult on a regular basis may be adversely affected in respect to language development, with the result that their language is more delayed than would otherwise have been the case. When they start school the fact that their language is delayed can make it harder for them to comprehend instructions or to sit and listen to a story. If they are also finding it difficult to hear, it is not hard to understand why they might start to misbehave. The cumulative effects are therefore very significant.

Since the hearing loss associated with glue ear can fluctuate from day to day or week to week, it can be difficult to diagnose it with accuracy. It may happen that on the day of the hearing test the child can hear well, whereas a week or so later the result would have been different. This fluctuation in hearing levels can be a source of frustration both for the children concerned and also for the adults working with them. For the children, they may hear clearly one week and then not hear as well. This period of not hearing as clearly may coincide with not feeling well either, if the cause is related to an infection, just as lingering catarrh can leave the sufferer with a slight headache all the time the catarrh persists.

For the class teacher the situation can be equally frustrating and confusing. Since the loss is usually only mild or moderate, the child may appear to have heard but then not respond appropriately. It may be that the child has misheard, having only heard part of the message clearly and possibly having missed parts of some words. When children are keen to please they sometimes resort to guessing in an attempt to get it right. Children with this type of loss will usually respond to their name, in fact it is often a useful strategy to call their name and gain their attention before speaking to them. Since they have responded to their name it is easy to assume that they have heard the rest of the message clearly as well, but this may not be true.

The effects of conductive hearing loss can be many and varied. The class teacher, especially the teacher of very young children, should be on the lookout for warning signs of a possible hearing loss and take action, reporting the signs to the child's parents or referring the child for a hearing test.

Indications of a possible hearing loss

- Child does not respond when name called. Hears name and simple instruction but not much else.
- Slow to respond to verbal instructions. Frequently asks for repetitions.
- Watches the speaker's face closely.
- Frequently seeks help from neighbours.
- Reluctant to answer questions – nods or shakes head instead.
- Speaks very softly or too loudly.
- Appears dull, uninterested or withdrawn.
- Appears inattentive or restless. Often seems to drift off. More responsive in a one-to-one or small group situation.
- Educationally behind especially in verbal subjects and literacy.
- Immature language (e.g. some word endings missed off, errors in grammar or weak vocabulary).
- Deafness in family.
- Persistent colds and catarrh, complaints about earache.

Management of behaviour

It is important to strike the right balance between making allowances if a child with a known history of hearing loss might not have heard and allowing an unacceptable pattern of behaviour to develop in which the child thinks it is not necessary to conform to the same patterns as are expected of the other children.

It is always wise to get the child's attention before speaking, even if this means saying their name. Waiting until you have secured the child's attention, including ensuring you have got their visual attention, will pay dividends. If you know that there are children in the class with a language delay, check that all the children have understood, rephrasing in simpler language and explaining key vocabulary if necessary.

Reducing background noise in the classroom will help all children to listen and encourage them to be quieter. This is even more important for children with some degree of hearing difficulty. There are more comments in Chapter 3 related to background noise as this has serious implications for hearing impaired pupils wearing hearing aids as well.

It can be much easier to manage the behaviour of a child who is experiencing difficulty in hearing in a smaller group, so, when there is a classroom assistant to help, use her to support a small group at times.

Having borne in mind that listening can be demanding and tiring and ensured that children are given regular breaks from listening, expect the same behaviour from children with a hearing loss as from the rest of the class. If they are developing habits which are unacceptable, stop them before these become entrenched and investigate the reasons behind the behaviour. It may be that the situation is too demanding and requires some modification to the way in which the whole class is managed.

Literacy

Literacy can cause particular problems for all children with hearing loss, including those with temporary fluctuating losses. While one should not expect that children will have problems it is helpful to bear a few facts in mind. Children with hearing loss may have difficulties which persist even after the hearing loss has passed.

During bouts of hearing loss children will hear less clearly. They may not detect the difference between some similar-sounding consonants, resulting in difficulties in phonic work. After the bout of hearing loss has passed, they may have missed some work which they need to catch up on, or they may need encouragement to translate their hearing into accurate listening. Some children do this automatically as their hearing returns, others need help.

Children who have had frequent bouts of hearing loss, or a hearing loss over an extended period of time, may have gaps in their vocabulary compared with other children of their age and their language development may be delayed. These factors mean that they may have less experience of language and vocabulary to bring to literacy, thus making it more difficult to use 'top–down' strategies which rely on knowledge of stories and their associated language and use of context. This is likely to be exacerbated in children from homes where it is not customary to spend a great deal of time in sharing books with children.

The approach to literacy, therefore, needs to take account of these potential difficulties and the possibility that they may persist. It has been found that older pupils who are referred for extra support at secondary stage frequently have a history of early hearing loss from which their literacy skills have never recovered.

Conclusion

An understanding of the possible implications of even a mild conductive hearing loss can give insight into how and why problems may develop in mainstream classes. Given the large numbers of children who are affected at some time, it is not possible to make special arrangements for them all, but some changes to overall class management may prove beneficial to all children. Teachers of young children, particularly in nursery and at Key Stage 1, should be alert to those children for whom a conductive hearing loss is presenting educational problems and take appropriate action.

CHAPTER 3

Deaf and hearing impaired pupils learning mainly via aided hearing

(NB: 'Deaf' is used here to refer to the full range of hearing loss)

Stephen Powers

Jeremy

Jeremy is 10 years old and attends his local primary school. He was born with a severe hearing loss but the cause is not known. There is no deafness in his family.

His deafness was not diagnosed until he was nearly two years old at which time his parents were concerned that he had not started to speak and also appeared not to understand what was said to him. Soon after deafness was diagnosed he was given hearing aids for both ears. His mother then began to receive twice-weekly visits from a Teacher of the Deaf for advice on managing Jeremy's use of hearing aids and his general development. During the visits the teacher also spent time with Jeremy, playing listening games and in activities designed to promote early language development. Jeremy gained considerable benefit from his hearing aids and clearly found great satisfaction others being able to hear. He responded well to sound and soon began to follow simple instructions. He also began to vocalise more and soon after his third birthday was producing his first words. His parents became convinced that the 'oral' approach was best for him.

At the age of four when he started attending his local school Jeremy was still significantly delayed in his language development compared to hearing children but his speech was intelligible and he was speaking in four and five word sentences ('he going to the shops', 'what you doing now?'). Soon after starting school Jeremy was given a radio hearing aid to use in class which helped him to hear the teacher better.

At primary school Jeremy continued to receive visits from the Teacher of the Deaf who often withdrew him from his ordinary class to work on language. Also a learning support assistant (LSA) was appointed to work with him during each morning. Most of the time she sat next to him in class, making sure he had understood instructions, helping him in his work, and in small group work encouraging other children to speak clearly and one at a time. Occasionally the learning support assistant took Jeremy out of class to do concentrated work on language and literacy skills.

Jeremy has made good progress. He is happy in school, is well accepted by other children and is an active and popular member of the school football team. His parents are now thinking about whether they want him to go to the local secondary school or to one a few miles away which has a resource base for hearing impaired children. They are worried about him travelling on his own on the bus.

Deaf children in the UK have been integrated (or 'included') in mainstream schools for a long time. The first 'units' for deaf children opened in London in 1947, but it is only in the last twenty years or so that there has been a major movement of deaf pupils away from special schools and into ordinary schools.

Deaf children are now educated in special schools for deaf children; in schools that have been specially 'resourced' for deaf children (these specialist provisions are sometimes called 'units') and on an individual basis in mainstream schools. Also, there are some deaf children educated in other types of special school. Leaving aside this last group, over 85 per cent of deaf pupils are now in mainstream, although the figure is much lower for those with 'profound' hearing loss.

Effective communication

For many people deafness is primarily a problem of communication. Indeed, the first concern of many mainstream teachers expecting a deaf child in their class for the first time is how they and the other pupils will communicate with the new pupil. For some the worry is that the child will use sign language and they will not be able to communicate easily with him or her. Most deaf children in mainstream schools communicate through spoken English, the use of residual hearing through hearing aids, and speech-reading. For those who do sign, support is provided both for the deaf pupils themselves and also for mainstream staff.

Charlotte

Charlotte is 14 years old and attends a secondary school which is specially resourced for deaf and hearing impaired pupils. She has a severe to profound sensori-neural hearing loss in both ears. There are twelve deaf pupils and two qualified Teachers of the Deaf at the school.

Charlotte went deaf a few weeks after her second birthday through meningitis. At that time she had quite a large vocabulary and was speaking in three word sentences. She was given two behind-the-ear hearing aids but it took her some months to get used to wearing them. At first she complained about the 'horrible sound' they made and there were frequent arguments between her and her parents over wearing them. However, once she became used to the hearing aids she became very dependent on them, although in most situations she also needed to watch people to understand what they were saying.

When Charlotte became deaf she had already make a good start at learning to speak. In view of this, and the fact that she appeared to gain significant benefit from her hearing aids, Charlotte's parents and the visiting Teacher of the Deaf were sure that the oral approach was best.

Between the ages of 5 and 11 she attended a primary school some way from where she lived which had a unit for deaf children. The local authority paid for a taxi to take her to and from school every day. Now she is in her local secondary school which also has a unit for deaf pupils. She has made good progress and reads well although she has a relatively poor general knowledge and vocabulary. She does not follow everything that is said in mainstream class and has particular difficulty understanding pupils' contributions to discussions. To help her keep up she is withdrawn for one lesson a week from English, History, German and French and given tutorial support by a Teacher of the Deaf. She is also supported in class for one lesson a week in Science and Geography.

Charlotte is a bright girl and is in the top set in most subjects. She is hoping to go to university to study architecture.

Hearing aids

Both pupils in the case studies wore hearing aids and relied on them. There are a number of different types of hearing aids but the ones the mainstream teacher is most likely to come across are personal hearing aids (usually worn behind the ear of the child as in the case studies, but on smaller children might be worn on the chest), and radio aids. Cochlear implants are a recent and special kind of hearing aid that a rapidly increasing number of deaf pupils are now wearing. These are discussed in Chapter 5.

Personal hearing aids are worn by the child all the time. Most children remove them at night, although some prefer to wear at least one on the grounds that they are like their ears and hearing people cannot switch off their ears. Waterproof aids are just coming onto the market, but most children will need to remove their aids when there is a danger of them getting wet, such as in the bath or swimming pool (a night in the airing cupboard has helped to dry out many an aid inadvertently left on!) Some children might also choose to remove their hearing aids during rough games, although it is not necessary for them to be removed during all physical activity and it may well be considered the danger of the pupil damaging either their ear or the hearing aid during sport is less than the danger that they will not hear a warning.

Personal aids work well when the speaker is close (within two metres) to the person wearing the aid and when both are in a quiet area. Unfortunately, in mainstream schools these ideal listening conditions are often not possible. Class teachers cannot be expected always to be standing or sitting next to the aided child, and a certain amount of noise in classrooms is difficult to avoid, such as the scraping of chairs (a very disturbing sound when heard through a hearing aid), or children talking (there are many occasions of course when teachers want children to be talking with one another). Furthermore, there can be noise from outside the classroom not under the control of the class teacher, for example from traffic or the playground.

In rooms with high ceilings and hard surfaces such as sports halls, assembly halls and science labs there is the additional problem of *reverberation* (where sound bounces off hard surfaces and becomes muddled). Also, if moulds (the bit that goes in the pupil's ear) are not fitting well hearing aids will be much less effective and will 'whistle'.

The following is a checklist of points to note when checking for noise in classrooms:

chairs scraping	banging desks
radiators	pens tapping
buzzing lights	playground noise
fans	noise from other classrooms
taps dripping	traffic
aircraft	noise from the playing field

Three tips when speaking to a hearing-aid wearer:
- be close;
- reduce the background noise;
- face the listener.

Radio aids were developed to help overcome some of the limitations of personal aids and indeed have revolutionised the hearing possibilities of pupils in mainstream schools. These aids comprise a small clip-on microphone worn by the teacher connected to a small radio transmitter which sends sound via radio signals to a small radio receiver worn by the pupil, connected to the pupil's personal aid. The radio aid goes a long way to overcome the problems created by the distance between the speaker and the hearing aid wearer, but the technology is complicated and class teachers need advice from Teachers of the Deaf or audiologists if it is to be used most effectively.

In summary, hearing aids are very important to many deaf children, they are an important link to the outside world. Unfortunately, even the best personal or radio hearing aids do not restore perfect hearing in the way that spectacles usually restore perfect sight. Amplified sounds may be unpleasant to listen to, and there may be distortion. Most pupils who are fitted with hearing aids wear them quite happily, but some pupils are reluctant to wear their hearing aids. This can be a particular problem in secondary schools where pupils are more concerned about their appearance. The class teacher should seek the advice of a Teacher of the Deaf to decide how best to manage such situations.

Some pupils' comments on hearing aids

Karl, 11 years old
I wear my radio aid because when someone is wearing the microphone I can hear them even when they are over on the other side of the room.

Hanif, 13 years old
I am very used to wearing aids. I feel with my hearing aids that I am a normal person but it is not very comfortable . . . When I do games with my hearing aid I find it is not very good because if I want to play rugby and I know that I am tough enough to play rugby I always worry about my hearing aids. I feel that I might break my aids or damage them . . . I also wear a phonic ear (a radio aid) which I find very helpful. It is like a walkie talkie but in my part of the walkie talkie I plug the speaker on to my ears (both of them) and it is much clearer.

Dawn, 11 years old
When I was quite little I had some hearing aids. I didn't like wearing them because the moulds whistled and they pinched me at the top of the ear. I used to blame my mum and complain about them. My mum was sick of me complaining . . . Without my hearing aids I can hear something but not clearly. If my mum was calling me from the bottom of the stairs and I was in bed I would not be able to hear her at all.

Mark, 15 years old
Every time I go out to play people say 'What's that in your ear?' I get embarrassed. Then I say 'a hearing aid'. Then they say 'What's it for'. Then I say 'What do you think it's for?' Nearly every day that happens.

Pupils who wear hearing aids may sometimes appear to hear well. Of course this may mean that the hearing aid is serving its purpose, but it can also be a source of confusion as the pupil may seem to have heard and then not respond appropriately. Some pupils pretend that they have heard to avoid the embarrassment of having to ask for a repetition or to cover up the fact that they cannot hear. Teachers of the Deaf frequently hear comments from mainstream teachers along the following lines:

'He's supposed to be deaf but he seems to hear me perfectly well!'

Remember, there is a difference between hearing a sound and clearly discriminating a sound. While it is true that many hearing aid wearers do hear relatively quiet sounds, in many cases they will not clearly understand what has been said. Most hearing-aid wearers are also dependent on speech-reading to be sure of the message.

Speech-reading

Almost all hearing-aid wearers also use speech-reading (lip-reading) to follow what is being said. Speech-reading is not easy, it depends on a knowledge of the grammar and vocabulary of the language (you can't speech-read a word that you don't know), it also demands great concentration and is very tiring to do over a long time. Also, there are different words that look the same to the speech-reader (for example, 'pear', 'bare' and 'mare', and 'to' and 'do') and some consonant sounds are very difficult to see at all because they are articulated back in the mouth (see if you can see the difference between 'are' and 'car' or 'great' and 'rate').

Deaf pupils have difficulties when they are required to look at sources of visual information, such as overhead transparencies, maps, and TV, at the same time as needing to speech-read the teacher. With static visual information the teacher can allow the pupil a few moments to look at it before they start talking (this is good practice for hearing pupils too). For TV or video the teacher should investigate whether subtitles are available, otherwise there might be a way for the deaf pupil to be given written notes to see before the lesson (the Teacher of the Deaf or LSA might be able to prepare these). If the pupil wears a radio hearing aid, then the transmitter can be connected directly to the video, which will enable the deaf pupil to hear the sound track more clearly. However, it is difficult to speech-read from the television and the face of the speaker may not even be visible.

Dictation poses other difficulties in that speech-reading inevitably slows down the process. Hearing children can write while they listen, deaf pupils cannot write and speech-read at the same time. Slowing down your rate of speaking can help, leaving pauses for the deaf pupil to catch up. It is good practice for the teacher to observe the deaf pupil during dictation and to wait until they look up to dictate the next phrase.

Suggestions for making speech-reading easier:
- face the hearing-aid wearer;
- don't cover your mouth;
- be in a position where your face is well-lit;
- speak clearly and at a normal pace;

- write new words on the board;
- present sources of visual information one at a time.

It is often also helpful to allow the deaf pupil to use a willing neighbour in class as a 'helper' for checking that instructions are understood (e.g. homework, page numbers) and possibly in copying dictated notes.

Suggestions for using TV, video or audio tapes:
- use subtitles if they are available;
- perhaps ask the Teacher of the Deaf or LSA to produce notes that the pupil could see before the lesson;
- in French oral assessments a speaker should play the tape and then speak the text to allow speech-reading.

Discussions in class

Whole-class discussions or situations where pupils are asked to discuss in small groups are particularly difficult for deaf pupils. Often they will say that they understand almost nothing of what the other children in the class are saying except for those sitting close by them. In some cases they might give up and might then become bored and restless and consequently either withdraw or become a nuisance and distraction to others. It is therefore absolutely vital that teachers try to include deaf pupils as much as they can in group discussions and question and answer sessions. For pupils who wear radio hearing aids, it is sometimes a useful strategy for the pupils to pass the transmitter round. While this can slow the pace down, it has the advantage of identifying the speaker for the deaf pupil and giving them a chance to watch them. Alternatively, the radio aid can be used with a conference microphone in which case the transmitter is placed on the table in the middle of the group discussing. This can work well provided there is little background noise or if the group involving the deaf pupil withdraws to a quiet area.

Suggestions for managing class discussions

With regard to the deaf pupil's understanding of the lesson:
- identify the speaker (by naming and pointing);
- repeat answers, questions and comments that come from the other pupils;
- control the discussion pace.

With regard to the deaf pupil's contributions to the lesson:

- be aware that deaf pupils won't hear everything that is said and therefore might make comments out of context (for example, answering a question which has already been answered);
- if deaf pupils have poor speech or expressive language they might be self-conscious about speaking in class.

Supporting other learning needs

The three main effects of deafness mean that:
- interpersonal communication is more difficult;
- there is often a delay in acquiring language;
- there is less information from the environment.

One of the main effects of deafness is on communication with others and this has been the focus of the chapter so far. We have seen that hearing aids and speech-reading together can go some way towards overcoming the difficulty but also that they are not the complete solution. But deafness affects other things besides communication.

Language

Many deaf pupils, but it should be stressed not all, are delayed in their acquisition of language skills. This might be apparent in difficulties in speech intelligibility, in vocabulary or grammar, or in skills in reading and writing. These difficulties are sometimes difficult to detect, for example a difficulty in understanding idiomatic language or knowing only one meaning of a word.

Hearing children learn to speak their first language through conversation with their parents and other caregivers. It is now well known that infants are not taught to speak by their parents but rather they acquire speech through using it and hearing it used in meaningful situations. Deaf children who are either born deaf or acquire deafness before the age of three years clearly face a more difficult task in learning a spoken language because they cannot hear clearly what is said. Unfortunately many deaf children start school at the age of five still in the early stages of learning their first language, and Teachers of the Deaf see this as one of their main areas of responsibility.

So, any curriculum for deaf pupils must have at its core a fundamental concern with the fostering of language skills. However, this is not to say that considerable time should be spent deliberately working on language. In fact, this appears to be the approach least likely to succeed. Rather, the most effective approach to fostering language development is by engaging children in relevant, meaningful and interesting conversation and activity. Webster and Wood (1989) have listed some of the helpful strategies to adopt when talking to deaf children.

Strategies for facilitating children's development of their first language:
- create a context for conversation; share activities which are relevant and meaningful to children's lives;
- show an interest in what the child is doing or talking about;
- talk with and not at children;
- encourage the child to question and to initiate dialogue;
- expand and clarify the child's intended meaning;
- allow time for the child to reply;
- avoid overuse of two-choice questions (e.g. 'Is that big or small?').

(adapted from Webster and Wood 1989)

In the light of this list many teachers might think that the mainstream classroom does not lend itself easily to the fostering of language development. For deaf children in the early stages of learning their first language this is probably true, and in these cases many Teachers of the Deaf would see the need for opportunities for small group or one-to-one work specifically to help develop language skills through conversation.

Environmental and other background sounds

Hearing is a distance sense that never switches off and as such it serves an important warning function. The fact that deafness results in less access to information from the environment also has other consequences. It has an heuristic effect in that deaf children have less information with which to construct their models of the world. Also, the fact that other people's conversations and TV and radio are not overheard can affect the rate of language acquisition and acquisition of general knowledge.

Some aspects of curriculum

Reading

The start of formal schooling for most children is marked by the beginning of a specific programme aimed at the development of literacy skills. This is no less true for deaf children. However, many of the reading schemes in infant schools assume a degree of linguistic competence that deaf children do not have and which, consequently, can make reading a fruitless, demoralising and potentially damaging exercise in linguistic and motivational terms.

The general delay in language development experienced by many deaf pupils during their school careers is the main reason for their difficulties in reading.

Furthermore, less access to the sounds of speech will make phonic work more difficult, and a weak general knowledge will affect 'top–down' skills.

Some feel that to gain access to the curriculum deaf children may need simplified reading materials. This is an area which needs careful attention, as over-simplification can render the text even less clear to the child than the fuller version, by removing the very redundancy within the material on which children operate. Modified texts can also restrict access to information, including new structures of language and vocabulary. Having said this, selected or prepared texts which take careful consideration of vocabulary and grammar can make all the difference to a poor reader, enabling them to be operating in the independence or instructional zones rather than the frustration zone.

Suggestions for developing reading skills in deaf pupils:
- make plenty of use of silent reading (reading aloud often introduces extra difficulties);
- use conversation and storytelling as foundations for literacy;
- make reading sessions enjoyable and stress-free;
- use a range of top–down and bottom–up approaches;
- don't keep stopping to correct language or pronunciation;
- consider the need to use modified texts.

Writing

Many deaf children have difficulty with their writing, particularly with grammar (for example, in the omission of articles and prepositions and errors in verb tense). This is often no more than a reflection of the child's delay in learning the grammar of spoken language. Sometimes the deaf child is frustrated in wanting to express complicated ideas without the language to do so – a result of a mismatch between the child's cognitive and language development.

For those working with young deaf pupils recent ideas about emerging literacy appear to be particularly useful. One principal feature of this approach is the strong rejection of the use of correction, other than self-correction. For example, if a child writes about a picture she has drawn:

'Mummy go work'   or   'Katie teddy bed'

. . . the teacher's response would not be to then correct the language and ask the child to rewrite as:

'Mummy's going to work' or 'Katie's putting the teddy to bed'

. . . but to consider the child's written ideas and their expression as a valid representation of their linguistic level. To ask the child to rewrite or copy the extended version would not, it is felt, be meaningful unless the child had reached a stage in their linguistic development where such additions could be attended to and were potentially part of their linguistic understanding. Indeed, such correction might contribute to the development of deviance in the child's writing.

Computer-aided approaches to literacy can be useful, but for children to derive real benefit the importance of collaboration with an adult is essential, rather than letting children just get on with it.

In many of the approaches mentioned here LSAs clearly have an important role to play.

Numeracy

There is nothing intrinsically different about deaf children's cognitive capacities which delays their acquisition of mathematical concepts. However, any linguistic delay, including a delay in acquiring literacy skills, will affect the learning of maths. After all, maths is taught through English, and it also has its own language which can be confusing when everyday terms are used differently.

An added difficulty for many deaf pupils is that they may not have been actively involved in using maths in real situations because of the difficulties in overhearing conversations about the basic mathematical aspects of life. There are clear implications here for teachers.

Study skills

In sessions with deaf pupils many Teachers of the Deaf and LSAs choose to work on study skills as much as directly supporting the subject content of mainstream lessons. Study skills often included are: reading for meaning; note-taking; exam techniques and essay writing. Also, particular emphasis is often given to encouraging older deaf pupils to adopt certain listening strategies, including:

- an adult approach to managing hearing aids;
- taking responsibility for testing aids, checking moulds, batteries, tubing;
- sensitive handling of situations where there are difficulties in understanding the teacher (including asking for repetition);
- arrangements for dictation, audio tapes, TV/video, etc.;
- coping with discussion groups.

Health and sex education

Much incidental information about sex passes many deaf children by because they miss out on jokes and stories, can't hear TV and might have weak reading skills. They may even not know the common terms for sexual body parts and sexual acts.

This problem of lack of information about sex can be exacerbated because parents may, because of communication difficulties, be even less inclined to discuss sexual matters with their deaf children than they are with their hearing children. It is perhaps the one area where parents are not willing to risk a situation where communication becomes difficult. There may also be a reluctance on the parents' part to recognise that their children are growing up and that the miracle is not going to happen, that their deaf child is becoming a deaf adult.

On this topic schools and teachers need to have a particular regard to the needs of deaf children. Of course, sex education should be approached in the wider context of the individual child's growth towards independence. This approach would include an appreciation of the responsibilities, values and emotional considerations associated with sexual behaviour.

Modifications to GCSE exam papers

Some years ago the British Association of Teachers of the Deaf established formal liaisons with Examination Boards to arrange procedures for modifying GCSE exam papers to meet the linguistic needs of deaf pupils. Certain special arrangements are now possible, including extra time, signing interpreters and language modification. Mainstream teachers should consult their visiting Teacher of the Deaf over this.

Working with other professionals

Mainstream teachers with a deaf pupil in their class often find they are working with other professionals who have a special responsibility to support such pupils. The other professional can be a visiting Teacher of the Deaf (a 'peripatetic' teacher), a Teacher of the Deaf based in the school resource base (or unit), or an LSA.

Teachers of the Deaf

Teachers of the Deaf are all qualified teachers with experience as mainstream teachers who have taken an additional training in the field of deaf education. They have often known the deaf pupil and family from a very early age.

The role of the supporting Teacher of the Deaf includes:
• giving general advice and support to mainstream teachers about hearing aids, about other equipment, about managing the listening environment, and about the educational and social implications of deafness;
• giving similar advice concerning individual pupils;
• working directly with pupils, either in or out of the mainstream class, checking hearing aids, developing language and speech skills, teaching literacy, supporting the school curriculum, providing pastoral support, and monitoring general progress;
• liaising with other professionals and the child's family.

Learning support assistants (LSAs)

There are now many assistants working alongside teachers in British schools and they come with a variety of titles, including 'classroom assistant' and 'support assistant'. The title recently preferred by our government is 'learning support assistant' (or LSA).

LSAs are not normally qualified teachers but will have received some training for their role. The class teacher has overall responsibility for the learning of all pupils in the class and the LSA works under their direction. Many teachers will have had no direct training in how to manage other adults in the classroom and might want some guidance about this.

A crucial feature of effective partnership between the class teacher and the Teacher of the Deaf or LSA is a clear understanding of roles. One major problem is that it takes time to work out an effective cooperative relationship, and time is often short.

How the Teacher of the Deaf or LSA might prepare a pupil for a mainstream lesson:
- check key concepts and key vocabulary;
- provide simplified texts (worksheets, books, etc.);
- provide notes about video or TV programmes;
- go through instructions (e.g. recipes, science experiments);
- provide supplementary texts for use in the mainstream class (e.g. maths worksheets);
- revise work just finished in preparation for the next step.

In-class support

There are a number of ways in which the extra adult in a classroom can offer support, including:
- working alongside the deaf pupil;
- acting as a note taker;
- team teaching with the class teacher.

Social development

Deafness can affect the social and emotional development of a pupil in a number of ways:
- difficulties in communication will make social interaction difficult;
- delayed language will affect the development of shared understanding and values;

- self-esteem can be affected;
- older deaf pupils might have worries about their identity;
- deafness can be very isolating.

Let us put ourselves for a moment in the position of a deaf pupil in a mainstream school. The following short story is by no means typical of all deaf pupils but it helps to highlight some of the possible problems.

Amy's story

Amy is a 14-year-old girl in a secondary unit (a resource base in a mainstream school). Just recently Amy and Dawn have been wanting to spend all their lunch times in the unit. Amy says that only Dawn can understand her. Amy writes in one of her English assignments:

As I am deaf I don't really have any friends because I am different to everyone else except Dawn. She and my family are the only people in the world who understand my life, being deaf and a hard worker trying to be like everyone else. Debra (a classmate) is a hard friend for me because she is very bright, and I have to work jolly hard to be like her. Miriam (a friend Amy met on holiday) is Dutch and is a good friend to me because as she is Dutch she is like a deaf person because she doesn't know any English and she sort of mimes what she is trying to say . . . I have no best friends just a few hard friends. Being deaf isn't all that fun.

We might regard the problems Amy is facing as not so different from the problems many of her hearing teenage friends will also be facing. Certainly there is some truth in this. However, there are a number of factors which compound the difficulties faced by the adolescent, and children of all ages, who are also deaf and in mainstream schools. These difficulties have nothing to do with deafness itself and in fact are often a consequence of other people's responses to the deaf pupil and the disabling barriers put up by institutions.

Strategies for fostering a deaf pupil's social and emotional well-being:
- create opportunities for successful and enjoyable learning and interaction;
- encourage full participation in curricular and extra-curricular activities;
- foster a positive attitude towards deafness in the school and the class;
- deal promptly and firmly with bullying and teasing;
- avoid excessive positive discrimination;
- avoid overprotection or favouritism;
- ask the educational psychologist to provide counselling if necessary;

- invite speakers in to talk about deafness to classmates (but include the Teacher of the Deaf/LSA and deaf pupils in this);
- monitor social aspects of deaf pupils' development.

Conclusion

Many class teachers of all ages and backgrounds have remarked that the presence of a deaf pupil in their class has caused them to review the efficacy of their teaching and, in their own words, to 'improve it for all the children in the class'. One such teacher of ten- and eleven-year-olds remarked that he felt his teaching had never been better than in the year when he had a profoundly deaf pupil in his class. Indeed, many mainstream teachers reading this chapter might have remarked that most of the suggestions for teaching deaf pupils are also useful for hearing pupils.

Some other comments from pupils

On noise
Sally-Anne, 12 years
Sometimes I hear the children outside doing games and I can't hear what the teacher says.

Peter, 16 years
It's background noise that's the main problem. I can't turn that down.

On the need for clear instructions
Georgina, 15
When the teacher goes on and on and I don't know what they say. And then sometimes they say 'Right, now you know what to do' and I haven't a clue what to do.

On speech-reading
Gwen, 14
I have a lot of problems with dictating now. A lot of teachers do dictating now instead of writing on the board and it drives me mad!

Elizabeth, 17
I had to listen to a lot of tapes and I can't hear the tapes. I can't lip-read the tapes.

On pretending to understand
Gwen, 14
Sometimes I say 'Yes' even when I don't understand, otherwise they (teachers) might think I'm stupid.

On using a neighbour
Cheryl, 13
My friend helps me, Tracy. She sits next to me, she tells me what's going on . . . 'What page is it?' She tells me '44' like that. She has a book and she points her finger under the writing for me.

On extra attention

Not all deaf pupils feel the same way about receiving extra attention and help.

Julie, 15
My form tutor is very nice. She helps me a lot. I like it when they help me.

Heidi, 15
I hate it when the teachers say 'Are you all right over there? Do you need any help?' It makes you feel stupid.

Mark, 16
I wouldn't like too much special attention during lessons. It's just I would have appreciated if they say come to me afterwards and just quiet-like said: 'Did you miss out anything?' And if I did I could have told them.

(Lynas 1986)

CHAPTER 4
Deaf children who sign

Susan Gregory

Gwen

Gwen is now 7 years old and profoundly deaf. She was born deaf and diagnosed before she was one year old and immediately fitted with hearing aids. She is a lively child, always moving about and inquisitive about the world around her. She has an older brother.

In her first year after diagnosis of her deafness, spoken language development was slow and both Gwen and her family became frustrated. When their visiting Teacher of the Deaf suggested the use of signing with Gwen, her family was delighted and felt this could make life easier for them all. Both parents started a course in sign language, but because of other commitments her father had to give it up and only the mother completed the course. Gwen went to a playgroup where some of the children used sign language and deaf adults were on the staff. Also, for a short time a deaf adult visited the family to help with signing skills. Gwen's older brother picked up signs very quickly from Gwen herself.

When it was time for Gwen to go to school her parents were concerned that her education should be in sign as that was her preferred way of communicating but it was also important to them that she should attend a mainstream school. Unfortunately this could not be the local school, which her brother attended, but she was able to go to a school with a signing unit using a Total Communication approach, where speaking and signing are used together. She travels every day by taxi and soon settled happily into school.

There are three other deaf pupils of her age and eleven deaf children altogether at the school. Gwen spends some time in a special base with a Teacher of the Deaf, and some time in a mainstream class. She follows well in the base with her Teacher of the Deaf. In this situation, either her Teacher of the Deaf or an LSA speaks and signs with her. However, she finds it more difficult in mainstream class. Here either her Teacher of the Deaf or LSA will repeat what the class teacher or other pupils have said, speaking and signing at the same time. This means she is often behind the other hearing children in the class in finding out what is happening. Sometimes it is difficult to concentrate, sometimes she is not sure where to look, at the Teacher of the Deaf or LSA, the class teacher, the other children or something the class teacher is pointing out.

Gwen likes to take part in class activities. She is always one of the first to raise her hand, even if she does not know the answer. Sometimes she falls behind in the lesson and her reply is to a question already answered. She also likes going to the front to address the class as a whole though often the other children cannot understand her. She finds reading and writing difficult, and does not seem able to use phonics as a way of learning to read. Often her writing is not grammatical in the English sense, for example she may write 'Shops I go Mummy'.

She gets on well with the other children in the class some of whom have learnt some signs. However she spends most of her time with her deaf friends.

This example of Gwen illustrates a number of aspects in supporting signing children in mainstream classes. She is young and has some difficulty in following in the mainstream class and even when she follows the communication to her may lag behind the communication to the hearing children. Because she uses the visual channel for so much, and it is essential for communication for her, she sometimes has difficulty in knowing how to divide her attention, in knowing what she should be looking at. The account also illustrates a number of more general social issues that may have implications for her education. Firstly, although both parents were willing to learn to sign, her mother is the better signer and thus communication is more often with her. This may have long-term implications for communication within the family. Secondly, although she attends mainstream school it is not her local school where children from her locality go and her friends tend to be deaf rather than hearing. However, before we can explore these in more detail it is necessary to understand something about signing and its use.

British Sign Language

A sign language is a visual gestural language. It uses the hands and facial expression in a systematic way to convey meaning. Sign languages have their own lexicon, or set of signs that refer to particular aspects of the environment. However, there is not a direct one-to-one correspondence between words and signs, some words need several signs to convey the meaning and likewise some signs can only be expressed by a number of words. Sign languages also have their own grammar or syntax. Meaning is expressed by the way in which signs are combined and used in conjunction with each other. Thus in the same way that 'John hit Mary' has a different meaning from 'Mary hit John', the same signs may be combined in different ways to convey different meanings.

A sign language is different from the spoken language of the country in which it develops since the grammar of sign languages is such that sign order and word order are different. Thus it is not possible to use a sign language and a spoken language simultaneously. Different countries have different sign languages, and in the UK the sign language is British Sign Language (BSL). This differs from other sign languages including that used in the United States, American Sign Language (ASL). Thus sharing a spoken language does not necessarily mean that the sign language will be the same. Despite the fact that there is evidence for the use of sign languages since there were families with a number of deaf members or since deaf people met together, sign languages have only been recognised as proper languages since the 1960s. The term 'British Sign Language' was coined as recently as 1976. Before that, the signing of deaf people was often seen as a form of mime and gesture and thus not suitable or even relevant for education. Now as a result of research in the area of linguistics it is acknowledged that BSL and other sign languages are proper languages and comparable with spoken languages in their ability to express and convey meaning.

Increasingly in special schools, but also in mainstream schools, some deaf children will be using signs, but they are not always used in the same way. Sometimes signs are used together with spoken language, speaking and signing at the same time. Sometimes a sign language is used, and this is never used simultaneously with speech.

Approaches to education using signs

In recent years, when signing was reintroduced into the education of deaf pupils, the initial approaches did not use full sign languages. Rather, signs were seen as a way of clarifying English. Signs were taken from BSL and used together with speech. You will have noticed that in the school Gwen attends, described above, signing and speaking are used simultaneously to communicate. Thus the signing used in these instances is not BSL, it could not be, as BSL sign order is different from English word order. A teacher speaks in English but introduces signs as she or he speaks as a way of clarifying the message, of providing a visual representation of it. This is called Sign Supported English (SSE) although other terms such as Manually Coded English (MCE) may be used (see Glossary). Usually only some of the message is signed, but there are systems where the attempt is made to sign every word (see glossary).

In mainstream schools, if signs are used, it is most likely to be SSE. However, in some educational settings full sign language is used. If this happens the child will be encouraged to develop the two languages, English and BSL, as separate languages. They will use the language that is usually easier for them to acquire, BSL, to support the development of their English. The languages will be used in different ways in the school. A child may have English as their preferred or first language or they may have BSL. If you would like to know more about this you are referred to the list of further reading at the end of the book.

Unfortunately the terminology that surrounds the various approaches to the education of deaf pupils who use signs is not clear, particularly as it relates to the use of the term 'Total Communication'. Total Communication originally developed as a philosophy which encompassed the use of any form of language or communication, spoken language, sign language, gesture, mime, drawing, in the education of deaf children. While this use is retained in some instances, the term is now more often used to refer to the use of SSE with deaf children. Thus a school or unit that describes itself as having a Total Communication approach is most likely to use signs and speech simultaneously, although some places use the term in its original meaning which covers a range of language and communication.

In educational settings where BSL and English are used as separate languages, the approach is known as a bilingual, or sign bilingual approach. This has been defined as 'an approach to the education of deaf children in which the language of the Deaf community (British Sign Language) and the language of the hearing community (English) are used' (Pickersgill and Gregory 1998). Often, in this approach, sign language is developed first to provide a firm basis for the development of spoken language and literacy. Reading and writing may be developed through contrasting the two languages.

Gwen

In the instance of Gwen described above, the approach used in school is Total Communication using SSE. However, it is likely that Gwen herself has developed some competence in BSL through her early exposure to sign language at nursery and through her contact with other deaf children.

There are a number of implications for the class teacher. In the mainstream class, because of the way in which information is conveyed to Gwen by her Teacher of the Deaf or LSA, there will be a delay for her in getting the message, it will not be at the same time as for the hearing children and she may not be ready to respond at the same time as other children. As mentioned earlier she will constantly be making decisions about where to look, particularly if visual material is being used in the lesson. It is important for the class teacher to make sure Gwen is attending to the right person or object and to indicate clearly what she should be looking at. Gwen will also need time to take in visual information, for example she cannot look at a picture and receive information about it at the same time. She may need extra time to look at the picture, receive information, look back at the picture and so on. If a class teacher is aware of this and paces the lesson accordingly it will be of great help to Gwen. It is likely to also help others in the class. As is often the case, good practice with deaf pupils can be good practice for all.

Earlier chapters have described how deafness may affect the development of literacy. With Gwen there may be an additional factor. She may use her knowledge of BSL to support her writing, particularly if she is not yet sure of the English. In the example of her writing that was given 'Shops I go Mummy' the influence of BSL sign order is apparent and it could be seen as a correct representation of a 'BSL sentence'. Rather than seeing this as a problem, it can be seen as an advantage, as her knowledge of BSL may be used as a way of explaining English structures, allowing Gwen to compare and contrast the two languages. This is likely to be carried out in conjunction with her Teacher of the Deaf.

While Gwen's speech may not be intelligible to the hearing children, her attempts to communicate and describe her own work should be encouraged. Often the children in the class, as happened with her brother, will develop ways of communicating, usually through a mixture of signs and speech. Her knowledge of signs should be seen positively, as one of her skills, and it may be useful to point this out to others in the class. Developing relationships between deaf and hearing pupils can have benefits for all, though the fact she spends most time with other deaf children means that the ease of communication they provide is important for her.

Raj

Raj is 14 and severely deaf. At primary stage he was in a unit using Total Communication. He is academically very able and for his secondary education has moved to a mainstream school with no unit. He has the support of a communicator who attends most, but not all, lessons with him. The communicator repeats what the teacher says but without using her voice, just lip patterns, and accompanies this message with signs. Sometimes Raj is attending to something else when she needs to sign to him and looks at her when the teacher has already said a few sentences. To save time, and to keep up with the lesson, she gives him a much reduced message. Raj has asked that when the class work in smaller groups the communicator leaves him to manage, as he prefers this. Raj continues to wear his hearing aid although at times he switches it off.

Because of the level at which Raj is working, terms are often introduced for which there is no specific sign, or the communicator is unfamiliar with the sign that should be used. In these instances she has to fingerspell the word which takes more time. Occasionally Raj finds a lesson difficult because a term is introduced that he himself does not understand. For example, in a mathematics lesson a timer was used to illustrate measuring duration, but because he was unfamiliar with the notion of 'timer' he found this lesson very difficult to follow.

If Raj were a member of your class a number of issues might arise. As with Gwen, Raj is using his visual channel for communication and all presentations in the lesson that occur visually, such as diagrams, charts, demonstrations and video. This means there is a constant problem as to where he should be looking. He may miss the beginning of what is said, or get a reduced message because he was late attending. As far as possible Raj should be encouraged to watch his communicator, particularly when very significant information is being conveyed.

For some technical terms there may not be a specific sign or the communicator might not know it. She will have to develop one, or fingerspell the word.

In fingerspelling each letter of English can be represented by a particular handshape. Thus English words can be put across by spelling them. Fingerspelling is used in SSE, and sometimes in BSL, although in BSL its use is mainly for names. Fingerspelling is a lengthier process as it involves producing each letter of the word on the hands. Thus the introduction of new terms, particularly technical terms or terms specific to the curriculum area being studied should be done with care and it is helpful if these are always presented in their written form as well as their spoken form, to reinforce the message.

Because of Raj's deafness, there are some aspects of general world knowledge he may have missed, ideas that hearing children pick up naturally that have passed him by. He may not be able to do something, not because he is intellectually unable, but because he is unfamiliar with the ideas discussed. For example, the word 'timer' may never have been used with him and his opportunity for overhearing, which is the way hearing children are likely to have acquired the term, may be limited. Thus when it is introduced in a lesson as an example to facilitate learning, Raj may be disadvantaged because he will have to understand and learn the term before he can use it.

As with Gwen, the class teacher and the communicator may be out of synchrony. Also Raj may receive a reduced message as the communicator tries to keep up with the lesson and thus abbreviates some things. The more the class teacher is aware of where Raj is looking and the information he is getting, the more she is able to support him.

Raj has taken responsibility for a number of issues himself and he manages the use of his hearing aid. He uses a radio aid and often prefers the class teacher, rather than the communicator, to wear the transmitter, particularly if the teacher does a lot of demonstration in the lesson as he needs to switch immediately to what she is doing. Thus when attending to the communicator, unless Raj switches off his aid, he may be receiving confusing messages. Also, since there is a time lag between the communicator's signing and the class teacher, he may miss the beginning of the demonstration and it is important that the teacher waits for him to attend. If the class teacher is aware of these points, it is possible to allow for the extra demands being made on the deaf pupil.

He also decides when he wants to use the communicator and likes her to withdraw from class discussion to allow him to participate. In these instances he will be reliant on his hearing aid and the same factors apply as in managing discussions with pupils who use hearing aids.

Mark

Mark is 11 years old and severely deaf. He attended his local mainstream primary school, where he was the only deaf child, with support from a learning support assistant. However, he made slow progress in the development of his spoken language and in other curriculum areas. There were concerns as to whether he would be able to cope with the demands of a mainstream secondary school where education was through spoken language. It was decided that he should attend a unit with a Sign Bilingual approach. He was disappointed at not going to the same secondary school as his friends from primary school, and is finding it difficult to make friends.

His sign language is developing slowly as he was previously educated through spoken language alone and knew no signs. He is currently taught some lessons in the unit and attends others in the mainstream school. In lessons in the mainstream school he is still uncertain as to whether he should use BSL or English to the class teacher. However his sign vocabulary is not yet developed enough for him to be able to access many curriculum areas.

A number of children are transferred from spoken language environments to signing environments because they fail to make progress with spoken language. While signing may assist them in the long term, they often have a great deal of catching up to do and it cannot be assumed that exposure to signs will provide a quick and easy solution. It will take time and specialised tuition for Mark to be able to benefit from the curriculum of the school. In mainstream classes, attention should be given to making material accessible through visual means and through the use of simple language, either BSL or English. The language of written work may need to be modified for him, either by the mainstream teacher or by a member of staff from the unit. There is no reason why his cognitive ability should be affected and thus every attempt should be made to stretch him academically given the constraints of the situation.

Ruth

Ruth is 6 years old. She is severely deaf and has deaf parents. She is a fluent user of BSL. She has a younger sister, Hayley, who is partially hearing and the family communicates through sign language. She is socially very confident and has many friends at school. They communicate through a mixture of signs and speech. She has started at her local primary school with support from an LSA who interprets the class activity into sign language for her.

Ruth is making good progress and is starting to read and write. Her LSA gives her a great deal of help in this and sometimes Ruth objects, as she wants to do things for herself. Her LSA sometimes finds it difficult to interpret what Ruth is signing to the class and so some of her contributions to lessons are missed.

Ruth's parents attend meetings held at the school and are very keen to receive information on how she is progressing. They spend a great deal of time looking at books with her and want to help her with her reading and writing. They have explained that reading and writing are very important in deaf families, as deaf people use reading in ways additional to hearing people, for example they use text telephones, and subtitles to access television programmes, thus they are concerned that her reading should develop well. While sometimes communication between school staff and parents is adequate, sometimes it is difficult for staff to fully understand them and they are not always sure Ruth's parents have understood them. This occurs particularly in discussing the errors Ruth makes in her writing.

Ruth's parents see themselves as members of the Deaf community. They do not consider themselves as disabled but rather members of a linguistic and cultural minority group. They are proud of their language and culture, and while they work in the hearing world they spend much of their leisure time with other deaf people. They want Ruth to be able to cope in the hearing world but also to be part of the Deaf community.

The issues posed by Ruth are slightly different from the other pupils described. She is fully fluent in her own language, BSL, with age-appropriate language, but her English is developing more slowly. She is learning to read and write in what is, for her, a second language. As with Gwen her writing often reflects her first language, BSL, and words are sometimes written in BSL sign order. As with Gwen, this should not be seen simply as incorrect English. Explanations should describe how the two languages are different and as far as possible build on her linguistic competence in BSL to develop her English.

Because she is the only child in her class with an LSA, she gets her undivided attention. This is sometimes too much and there is a danger Ruth could become too reliant on her. Communicators and LSAs need to be encouraged to withdraw, even if it means they are apparently doing nothing, so that pupils learn to work things out for themselves, even if they have to struggle at times.

The relationship with her parents needs to be considered. The possibility of using sign language interpreters for some of their visits to the school must be considered so they have full access to information about Ruth and can make their own concerns known. If this does not happen, they do not have equal opportunities to participate in Ruth's education, compared with other parents.

The decision will have to be made as to whether Ruth should stay in mainstream or attend a school with a Sign Bilingual programme. Because she is severely deaf rather than profoundly deaf and a competent communicator, she may well develop English to a level that will allow her to benefit from continuing in mainstream, although she or her parents may prefer her to be in the company of other deaf children.

In summary, a few points can be made that apply in general to signing environments:

- The pupils need clear guidance as to where to look. If there are a number of sources of information it can be difficult to decide. This applies particularly to classroom discussions.

- If visual materials are used, deaf pupils will need time to look before communication continues, as they are using the visual channel for information and communication. If a teacher wants to comment on something that is presented visually they should be careful to allow pauses for the deaf pupil to check the visual information.
- The signed message may be behind the spoken message and the pupil needs time in the lesson to catch up so they can participate fully.
- New terms may present problems as the child may be unfamiliar with them or there may not be a sign for them.
- The use of hearing aids needs careful consideration so messages are not confused.
- Social relationships need to be considered and deaf and hearing pupils encouraged to interact and collaborate. Signing should be seen as an interesting way of communicating, a skill to be learnt rather than a barrier to deaf – hearing communication.
- Deaf pupils should be seen in terms of their strengths, in their ability to access the curriculum through a different modality and even language from other pupils, rather than simply deficient in their ability to hear.

CHAPTER 5

Children with cochlear implants

Susan Gregory

Stephen

Stephen was 7 years old when he contracted meningitis. Before then he had been a lively child, average in his school work, and a child who enjoyed sport. He is the elder of two boys in the family. The meningitis was a severe shock to the family; no young person in the immediate family had been really ill before. At one time they wondered whether he would survive; he did make a full recovery but was left with severe hearing impairment.

His behaviour changed at this time. He became withdrawn, did not join in class activities and stopped enjoying sport. At first his friends were kind and tried to include him in their activities but they soon lost interest. His parents, and in particular his mother, became very protective, when he was not at school he was always with one of them. He watched a lot of television but not in an involved or interested way as before, rather somewhat passively.

It was suggested to the family that they should consider a cochlear implant. At first they resisted the idea, their recent experience of hospital had been very frightening and they were most reluctant to put their son, who had already had a serious illness, through such a major operation. However, as the effect of the deafness became more apparent and Stephen became more withdrawn, they felt they should consider it further. They went through a long period of discussion and assessment with the cochlear implant team to ensure that the operation was appropriate for Stephen. They were disappointed that the cochlear implant team could not be more definite about the outcome, and in fact emphasised that they should not expect too much. They had hoped from some of the things that they had heard about the 'bionic ear' that it would cure the deafness, that Stephen would hear again as he used to. Although they were told he would almost certainly regain some hearing, they were also told it would not be a 'cure'.

In the end they decided to go ahead. A factor that pushed them into a decision was that they were told that meningitis could damage the cochlea and to delay could create problems. The time leading up to the operation was extremely stressful for them. They prepared Stephen as well as they could through discussion, drawings, hospital visits and he seemed accepting of the process. His younger brother started to show signs of stress and became more demanding of attention. The day of the operation was, for them, the worst in their life. They took him to the hospital and settled him in, but did not know what to do with themselves during the time he was in theatre. They wondered over and over again whether it was right to let him undergo such a major operation. They tried not to think about the operation itself, and the fact it involved drilling into the skull. The time did pass, and they were pleasantly surprised to see how well Stephen had coped with the operation. He was able to return home after two days and he made a good recovery, far more quickly than they had anticipated.

The next major event for them was the initial tuning. At the back of their minds the parents had seen this as 'being switched on' and that the hearing would flood back. In reality it was not like this and Stephen appeared bemused more than anything else, although towards the end of the session he started to show he was aware of some sounds. Within weeks though there was a dramatic change. Stephen could hear more and more sounds although he could not always immediately interpret what they were. He needed a great deal of practice in listening, using everyday sounds, but also material with which he was familiar such as books and other reading materials. With encouragement he became more and more able to interpret what he heard. He joined in conversation, and some time later he was able to speak on the telephone. Throughout this period he attended the hospital on a number of occasions for retuning of the device.

He began to cope better at school, although it went in phases. Sometimes he was fully involved; sometimes he seemed to miss a lot. It was always more difficult for him to hear when there was background noise. He became easily annoyed, often because he had missed something that was said. Because he was able to respond to speech most of the time, often people did not appreciate that he did also miss a lot and needed to concentrate if he was to hear.

This long case study is included because it introduces a number of the issues that relate to children with cochlear implants. Many of them may not seem to be directly issues for the classroom, but an understanding of them may help in classroom management. You might like to reflect for a while about the role that you, as a class teacher, may have in this situation, or the times when knowledge about what is happening may be useful.

Clearly the impact of meningitis on a child which results in deafness will be traumatic. A child may feel a sense of confusion or even loss. The family may be coping with the child and their own feelings about the meningitis. There may be relief that the child survived but concern as to how to cope with the new situation. This stress may affect other members of the family, particularly siblings. The decision as to whether the child should have an implant may be a difficult one. An implant operation is major surgery, and the parents ultimately take the decision for the child to undergo surgery. They may have to consider the fact that it is not a life-saving procedure, it is elective surgery. In addition, there is uncertainty about the outcome. The child may, or may not, make good progress. Even if he does, there will always be situations that are more difficult for him than for hearing children. He will have difficulty with background noise; he will have to concentrate to make sense of what is going on. He may miss things, which can be frustrating.

For the classroom teacher this raises a number of issues. Many of these are similar to those for other children with hearing loss and some of the ideas of classroom management covered elsewhere in this book are relevant, as a child with a cochlear implant is a deaf child who has a technological aid to support his or her hearing. However, there are other areas where some knowledge may be useful in order to make best use of the implant. These include supporting the child through the period of transition and providing reassurance. There is also the need to build on the skills the child already has and, in the early stages in particular, to provide opportunities for listening and for making sense of sounds in familiar contexts. The child may need to be told, or shown, the source of the sounds he hears. Being informed about cochlear implants will also facilitate good classroom practice and below are some common questions that have been be raised.

What is a cochlear implant?

A cochlear implant aims to stimulate the auditory nerve directly to give a sensation of hearing. It is an electronic device providing direct electrical stimulation to the cochlea though electrodes. The internal parts are the receiver and electrodes which are implanted surgically. The external parts are the microphone, speech processor and transmitter.

How does it work?

The microphone which is at ear level picks up speech or other sounds. The speech processor converts this to electrical signals which are conveyed via the transmitter through the skin to the implanted receiver and then to the electrodes.

What is its effect?

The device has to be tuned, which usually takes place over a period of time, starting about a month after the implant operation. It provides a sensation of sound which is not the same as hearing people hear. It has been described as being like Daleks under water. Children with implants have to learn to use their device, to make sense of the sensation they receive.

How common are they?

About 10,000 children have been implanted worldwide, in the UK 1,000 children had been implanted by the end of 1998. About 200–300 children a year may be considered suitable for implantation.

What can go wrong?

In a very small minority of children things can go wrong at the implant stage and the child may need to be reimplanted. Later on the device may fail. A classroom teacher is unlikely to have responsibility for checking the device. However, any changes in the child's behaviour could indicate something is wrong with the implant and this should be conveyed to the child's Teacher of the Deaf. The sort of changes might be:

- signs of discomfort associated with the implant;
- damage to the implant;
- change in general behaviour, such as an increase in bad behaviour;
- avoidance of communication;
- change in ability to perceive or produce speech;
- change in response to environmental sounds.

Does having an implant affect participation in sports, swimming, etc.?

You should discuss any concerns that you have with the child's Teacher of the Deaf. However, most sports are acceptable, except those where there is a possibility of a serious blow to the head. Swimming should not present a problem providing the external parts of the system are removed. Static electricity can damage the implant although this will not hurt the child. In particular, before playing on plastic play equipment such as plastic slides or bouncy castles the child should remove the speech processor and headset. The same applies if the child is working with static electricity at school (as part of the National Curriculum).

Stephen, described in the study above, had acquired spoken language in the usual way and was a competent user of the language. The issue for him was to help him make sense of what he heard, to use his previous knowledge to support the use of the implant.

Of course, not all implanted children could previously hear. Although when the operation was first carried out on children in 1989, it was with those who had a hearing loss as a result of some illness or trauma; since 1991 they have also been used with children who were born deaf. Initially this was with children with profound hearing loss, where conventional aids were of little use. Now, however, their use is being extended to those who are less deaf.

Sarah

At 5 years of age Sarah is starting at her local infants school with her friends. Her older sister attends the same school, and Sarah has been looking forward to going to school for some time. Although she is a bit reserved on her first day, she soon settles down. Sarah has a cochlear implant.

Sarah was born profoundly deaf, and had little useful hearing. She was diagnosed at 9 months as a result of a Health Visitor assessment, although her parents had had some concerns before that. The grandmother saw a television programme about implants, and was impressed by what she saw. She encouraged her son and daughter-in-law to go to their GP and ask about the possibility of an implant. They were referred to the cochlear implant team and went through the long period of assessment. Sarah was seen as a good candidate, and her parents were confident it was the right decision for her family. She had her implant just before her second birthday, relatively early, as children are rarely implanted under the age of eighteen months.

They were disappointed when Sarah was first 'switched on', as she seemed distressed by the sensation she was experiencing. It had to be abandoned that time. However, later tuning sessions gave her a signal with which she was comfortable and she began wearing the speech processor happily, listening to sounds in her environment and responding to the sounds of speech. What various sounds meant had to be explained to her, she had to be shown it was the telephone, or the vacuum cleaner that created the sensation that she heard. Language development progressed slowly at first but by the time she started school at the age of 5, she had developed spoken language appropriate for her age. She could cope easily in one-to-one situations although she found it more difficult as a member of a group.

Her local Teacher of the Deaf visited her regularly at school and provided support to the school. She was also visited by a number of professionals from the cochlear implant team at the hospital who gave advice and carried out a number of different assessments with her.

What does the teacher need to be aware of as Sarah starts school? You may like to reflect on the points that you would want to consider.

The role for the classroom teacher here would be similar to any teacher with a child with a significant hearing loss and a number of issues have been discussed in the other chapters in this book. However, the teacher should also be aware of some of the issues about cochlear implants mentioned above. It is also helpful for the teacher to recognise that, although Sarah can hear sounds, she may not be able to interpret them and may need some help with this.

As this case study shows, a child with a cochlear implant may not only be of concern to the local Service for Hearing Impaired Children but also to the cochlear implant team. There may be a number of professionals visiting and their relative roles may need to be considered. They may make demands on the school in terms of time spent with the child, time spent with staff and use of rooms. This may seem even more significant if there are two children in the class with an implant and they have been implanted by different teams, both of which visit.

Claire

Claire is nearly 7 years old; she is an only child and quite shy. She is transferring to her local infants school. Previously she attended a unit for hearing impaired children some distance away. The unit had a Total Communication policy and Claire communicates well through signs. Following a cochlear implant at the age of four years, she is now beginning to make good use of her hearing and to develop some spoken language. Her literacy skills are good and she reads and writes well for her age.

Claire's parents are happy for her to sign and use signs with her at home. However they also feel that good spoken language is important for her and consider that a mainstream school where all communication is through speech will provide the best opportunity for this to develop.

Claire's teachers may be concerned about how she will settle at the new school. She has moved from a signing environment, with which she is familiar, to a non-signing environment which is new to her. It will be important to familiarise her with school routines. Initially she should not be expected to pick up information through speech. It will be important to build on her good literacy skills and to encourage her in the areas in which it is known she is competent. Claire will need to learn to listen and use the sounds she hears. She will need opportunities for communication in contexts where the meaning is clear so she can develop her spoken language, using the communication and language skill that she has developed through the use of signs.

While her signing is not now used in class, she should not feel that communicating that way is inferior and her achievement in being able to sign should be recognised. It will be important to explain to the children in her class about deafness, and about her implant. Maybe they should learn some signs and maybe she will enjoy showing them some or showing her teacher who can then explain to the class. If she can fingerspell, this may be a useful skill to introduce to the class, it may also help their reading and spelling too!

Paul

Paul is 9 years old and he was born profoundly deaf and received his implant when he was 6 years old. He attends his local primary school in accordance with the policy in his area. Before his implant he could say only a few words. He coped with school by copying the others around him, and became skilled at this. Since his implant he has become more aware of environmental sounds and responds enthusiastically to the sound of the buzzer indicating the end of lessons, etc. However, he has made little progress in his language development. His parents, who initially were very enthusiastic about the implant, have now become discouraged.

This is not an unusual situation where a child has been implanted relatively late and, for whatever reason, is making little progress with his implant. However, his implant was only three years ago and for many implanted children it takes at least two years before the benefit is apparent. In school it would be important to encourage him in his response to the sounds he does hear and respond to appropriately. However, there is a need to review his future placement, and careful records kept by the class teacher will be an important resource in doing this.

Conclusion

Many of the skills needed to work with children with cochlear implants are similar to those needed with other children with hearing losses. However, there are a number of issues which may be different, and are useful to consider.

- The time of implantation may be very stressful for the parents and other members of the family.
- The benefits of the implant may become apparent very slowly; there may be little evidence of any improvement in the early months.
- Some children will have been able to hear before their implant and may have already developed competence in language.
- Children with implants may be the focus of attention, not just of the local Service for Hearing Impaired Children but also of the cochlear implant team.
- Children who transfer between schools after implantation need particular consideration, especially if there is a change in educational approach.
- There are some safety and care factors that need to be taken into account for children with implants.

Postscript

While implants are regarded by many as a major development and innovation in the care and education of deaf children, others have expressed concerns about them. It may be useful to be aware of these.

Some are concerned about the cost, and whether the benefits are justified by the expense. A major research project is looking at the benefits and this will provide us with some evaluation of their effectiveness and benefit. Others express this by seeing a disproportionate amount being spent on children with implants compared to other children with hearing loss, although it is doubtful that if there were no implants this money would be used for deaf children.

There is concern about carrying out major surgery on a child who is not ill, and who does not need surgery to remain healthy. A further related concern is that the emphasis on surgery makes deafness a medical issue, and furthermore the appropriate treatment is to restore hearing as far as possible, rather than looking at the deaf child as a deaf child and considering the best way to facilitate their development and educate them. The Deaf community, in particular, feel that cochlear implants reinforce a notion that deaf people are defective in some way, and rather than seeing their language and way of life as a strength, feel it is inferior and second best.

Glossary

Bimodal approach
A more appropriate term for total communication, where spoken language and signs are used simultaneously.

British Sign Language (BSL)
The sign language used in the UK.

Finger spelling
The representation of the letters of the alphabet on the hands. It can be used as part of BSL and is commonly used for names or new terms.

Manually-Coded English (MCE)
See Sign Supported English.

Sign bilingual approach
An approach to the education of deaf children which uses the sign language of the deaf community and the spoken language of the hearing community.

Signed English (SE)
The use of English but where every word is signed and grammatical features marked. Also known as Signing Exact English (SEE).

Sign language
A visual gestural language which has its own grammar and lexicon. These differ from those of spoken language.

Sign Supported English (SSE)
The use of the English language with some signs taken from the lexicon of BSL. Also know as Manually-Coded English (MCE).

Total communication

The term commonly used for an approach to the education of deaf children that uses English supported by signs. Originally the term was used to refer to a philosophy where all forms of communication, including sign language, were used with deaf children.

References and further reading

Ballantyne, J. C. (1992) *Deafness*, 5th edn. London: J. and A. Churchill.

Gregory, S. *et al.* (1998) *Issues in Deaf Education*. London: David Fulton Publishers.

Lynas, W. (1986) *Integrating the Handicapped into Ordinary Schools – A Study of Hearing Impaired Pupils*. London: Croom Helm.

Mahshie, S. N. (1995) *Educating Deaf Children Bilingually*. Washington, USA: Gallaudet University Press.

McCormick, B., Archbold, S. and Sheppard, S. (eds) (1994) *Cochlear Implants for Young Children*. London: Whurr Publishers.

Pickersgill, M. and Gregory, S. (1998) *Sign Bilingualism*. Wembley: Adept Press (A LASER Publication).

Webster, A. and Wood, D. (1989) *Special Needs in Ordinary Schools: Children With Hearing Difficulties*. London: Cassell.

Index